WHAT WENT WRONG?

The Challenger Explosion

CORE EVENTS OF A SPACE TRAGEDY

by John Micklos Jr.

Consultant:
James Gerard
Aerospace Education Specialist (Retired)
NASA—John F. Kennedy Space Center,
Florida

CAPSTONE PRESS
a capstone imprint

Fact Finders Books are published by Capstone Press,
1710 Roe Crest Drive, North Mankato, Minnesota 56003
www.capstonepub.com

Library of Congress Cataloging-in-Publication Data
Micklos, John.
  The Challenger explosion: core events of a space tragedy / by John Micklos Jr.
    pages cm.—(Fact finders. What went wrong?)
  Includes bibliographical references and index.
  Summary: "Explains the Challenger explosion, including its chronology, causes, and lasting effects"—
Provided by publisher.
  ISBN 978-1-4914-2046-1 (library binding)
  ISBN 978-1-4914-2221-2 (paperback)
  ISBN 978-1-4914-2236-6 (eBook PDF)
1. Space vehicle accidents—United States—Juvenile literature. 2. Challenger (Spacecraft)—Accidents—Juvenile literature. I. Title.
  TL867.M53 2015
  363.12'4—dc23   2014036882

Editorial Credits
Katy Clay, editor; Jenny Loomis, editor; Bobbie Nuytten, designer;
Wanda Winch, media researcher; Charmaine Whitman, production specialist

Photo Credits
Corbis: Bettmann, 7; Courtesy Ronald Reagan Library, 9; Getty Images: Hulton Archive/Keystone, 26, MPI, 24, 25; NASA, cover (all), 5, 11, 12, 21 (bottom), 29, NASA: History Office, 21 (top), NASA: Johnson Space Center, 1, 6, 13, 14, 15, 18, 19, NASA: Kennedy Space Center, 8, 22, 23, 28, NASA: GFSC/Arizona State University, 27; National Archives and Records Administration, 17; Shutterstock: Eliks, blue dot design, nienora, stars background, Rusian Gi, halftone dot design

Primary source bibliography
Page 6—"The Challenger Accident: Challenger timeline." www.spaceflightnow.com/challenger/timeline/.
Page 9—"NASA: President Reagan's remarks following the loss of the Space Shuttle Challenger and her crew." www.nasa.gov/audience/formedia/speeches/reagan_challenger.html.
Page 20—"Report of the Presidential Commission on the Space Shuttle Challenger Accident: Chapter IV: The Cause of the Accident." www.history.nasa.gov/rogersrep/v1ch4.htm#4.1.
Page 20—"Report of the Presidential Commission on the Space Shuttle Challenger Accident: Chapter V: The Contributing Cause of the Accident." www.history.nasa.gov/rogersrep/v1ch5.htm.
Page 29—Kohler, Robert T. I Touch the Future: The Story of Christa McAuliffe. Random House, 1986.

Printed in the United States of America in North Mankato, Minnesota.
062017   010595R

Table of Contents

Five. Four. Three. Two. One. Audiences at the Kennedy Space Center in Florida counted down with Mission Control. They cheered as the space shuttle *Challenger* roared into motion at 11:38 a.m. on January 28, 1986. Flames shot out of the bottom of the solid rocket boosters (SRBs). The giant shuttle cleared the launch tower and rose into the cloudless sky.

Onlookers shivered in near-freezing temperatures. Due to the unusual cold, ice had formed on the launch pad. Scientists at **NASA** worried that the ice could damage the shuttle. They pushed back liftoff two hours from the scheduled time of 9:38 a.m. That left more time for the ice to melt as the temperature slowly rose.

A Delayed Liftoff

Challenger's liftoff had already been pushed back several times. The shuttle had originally been scheduled to launch on January 22. Bad weather delayed a previous shuttle mission, which pushed back the timeline for *Challenger's* flight. Equipment problems with a broken bolt on the hatch door pushed back the launch an additional day.

NASA—the government agency that runs the U.S. space program; stands for National Aeronautics and Space Administration

On January 28, 1986, the space shuttle *Challenger* had its 10th launch. It had successfully completed nine previous missions.

"Obviously a Major Malfunction ... "

After 24 successful flights, shuttle missions seemed almost routine. In fact most missions received limited media interest. But this launch featured something new. For the first time the shuttle's seven astronauts included a civilian. Christa McAuliffe was aboard as the nation's first Teacher in Space. She was scheduled to teach two lessons from space during the mission.

Because interest was so high, CNN televised the launch live. At first everything seemed normal. At 70 seconds after liftoff, flight commander Francis R. Scobee said, "Roger, go at throttle up."

Three seconds later pilot Michael J. Smith said, "Uh oh." At that instant spectators on the ground saw what looked like a fireball. Then clouds of smoke poured from the spacecraft. Onlookers gasped in horror as they realized something was wrong. McAuliffe's parents, husband, and children were in the audience. So were students from her school. "Obviously a major **malfunction**," said Mission Control.

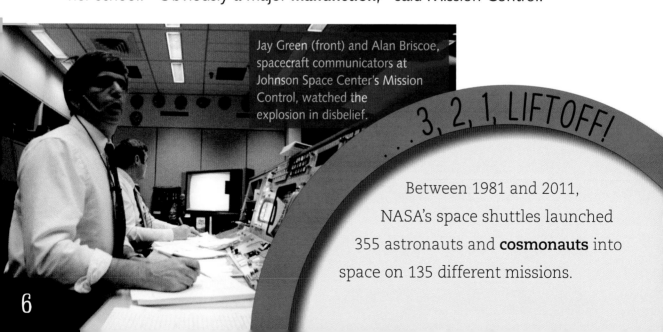

Jay Green (front) and Alan Briscoe, spacecraft communicators at Johnson Space Center's Mission Control, watched the explosion in disbelief.

... 3, 2, 1, LIFTOFF!

Between 1981 and 2011, NASA's space shuttles launched 355 astronauts and **cosmonauts** into space on 135 different missions.

Onlookers reacted with shock and sadness as the shuttle exploded in the sky above.

malfunction—a failure to work correctly

cosmonaut—a Russian astronaut

Just 73 seconds after liftoff, the *Challenger* flight ended in tragedy. The SRBs split off in a fiery blast. The **orbiter** part of the shuttle began to break apart. About three minutes later, the crew **compartment**, located inside the orbiter, crashed into the Atlantic Ocean. All seven astronauts died. **Debris** from the shuttle rained into the ocean for more than an hour.

Within hours people worldwide knew of the disaster. President Ronald Reagan praised the astronauts' bravery. He vowed to find out what had caused the accident. He promised that the shuttle program would continue once the safety of future flights could be guaranteed.

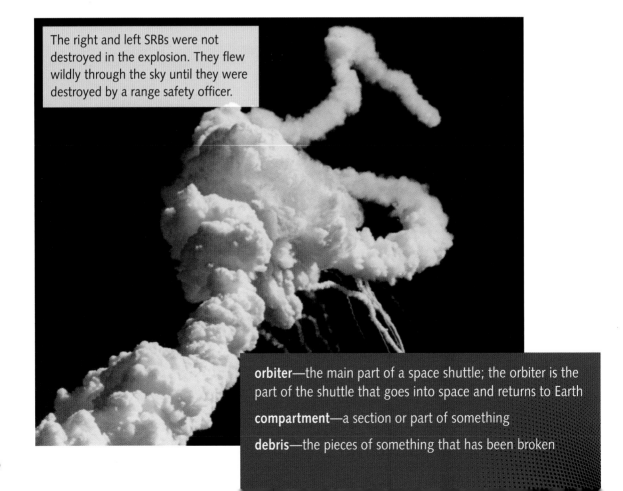

The right and left SRBs were not destroyed in the explosion. They flew wildly through the sky until they were destroyed by a range safety officer.

orbiter—the main part of a space shuttle; the orbiter is the part of the shuttle that goes into space and returns to Earth

compartment—a section or part of something

debris—the pieces of something that has been broken

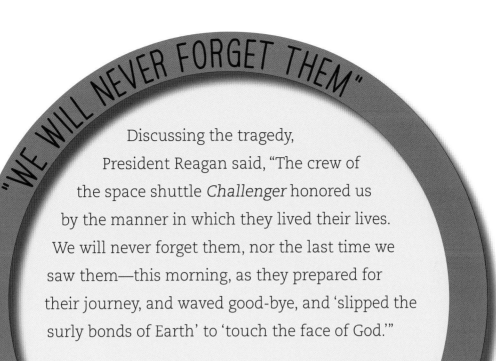

"WE WILL NEVER FORGET THEM"

Discussing the tragedy,
President Reagan said, "The crew of
the space shuttle *Challenger* honored us
by the manner in which they lived their lives.
We will never forget them, nor the last time we
saw them—this morning, as they prepared for
their journey, and waved good-bye, and 'slipped the
surly bonds of Earth' to 'touch the face of God.'"

President Reagan (third from right) and his staff watched a replay of the *Challenger* explosion on January 28, 1986. The annual State of the Union address had been scheduled for that evening. The address was cancelled so the president could discuss the tragedy instead.

In less than two minutes, the shuttle program went from triumph to tragedy. What had happened? How had the mighty spacecraft failed?

CHALLENGER CREW MEMBERS

Crew members on the *Challenger* flight included (front row, from left) Michael J. Smith, Francis R. (Dick) Scobee, Ronald McNair, (back row, from left) Ellison Onizuka, Christa McAuliffe, Gregory Jarvis, and Judith Resnick.

Challenger Tragedy Timeline: January 28, 1986

11:38 a.m.: *Challenger* launches.

11:39 a.m.: Commander Scobee suggests all is well. Seconds later Smith first mentions that something might be wrong. At that point the SRBs ignite and the orbiter begins to break apart.

9:38 a.m.: Original launch time of 9:38 a.m. pushed back due to ice on the launch pad.

9:30 a.m. . . . . 11:30 a.m . . . .

11:42 a.m.: The crew compartment where the astronauts sit crashes into the Atlantic Ocean.

5:00 p.m.: President Reagan addresses the nation about the *Challenger* tragedy.

11:40 a.m. .... **5:00 p.m.**

Within one week President Reagan formed a team to find out what caused the *Challenger* tragedy. Former U.S. Secretary of State William Rogers led the **commission**. Astronauts Neil Armstrong and Sally Ride joined the commission. So did engineers and other experts.

The group, called the Rogers Commission, spent several months reviewing mission data and videotapes of the shuttle's short flight. They ran tests and evaluated data. They studied recovered wreckage from the shuttle. They considered all possible problems that could have caused the spacecraft to fail.

The Rogers Commission found that the tragedy was caused by a rubber part called an O-ring. O-rings sealed the joints between sections of the shuttle's SRBs. They prevented hot gases from leaking through the joints as the hot rocket **propellant** burned.

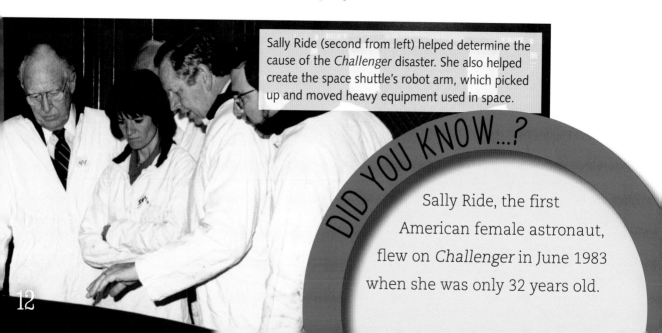

Sally Ride (second from left) helped determine the cause of the *Challenger* disaster. She also helped create the space shuttle's robot arm, which picked up and moved heavy equipment used in space.

DID YOU KNOW...?

Sally Ride, the first American female astronaut, flew on *Challenger* in June 1983 when she was only 32 years old.

But the O-rings had a flaw. The pressure of takeoff caused the seals to **compress** and shift slightly. The shift allowed gas to leak through. In most cases the O-rings quickly settled back into place. Some earlier launches had shown signs of O-ring **erosion**. Morton Thiokol, Inc. (MTI), the company that built the SRBs, was working to fix the problem.

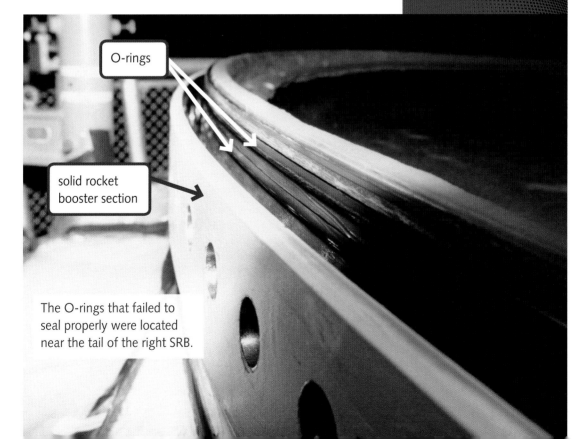

O-rings

solid rocket booster section

The O-rings that failed to seal properly were located near the tail of the right SRB.

Go Fever

Engineers at MTI worried that the O-rings would become hard and brittle in the cold weather and not resettle as quickly. They warned supervisors against launching *Challenger* in temperatures below 53 degrees Fahrenheit (11°C). That was the lowest temperature for any previous liftoff. Staff at NASA and MTI knew January 28 would be a cold day. They discussed pushing back the launch once again. But would the lower temperature really make a difference? No one knew for sure.

After all the liftoff delays, NASA felt the pressure to continue the *Challenger* launch as planned. Some people call this pressure "go fever." Without actual data proving danger, NASA officials decided to move ahead with the launch.

The temperature on January 28 was around 35 degrees Fahrenheit (1°C). The engineers' fears proved correct. Videotape of the launch showed puffs of black smoke beside the right-hand SRB during liftoff. The cold weather prevented the O-rings from sealing completely. Without a proper seal, escaping fuel damaged the booster. Still, everything appeared fine during the first 30 seconds of the flight.

Although the cold temperature contributed to the *Challenger* disaster, the ice buildup on the launch pad did not play a role in the accident.

engineer—a person who uses science and math to plan, design, or build

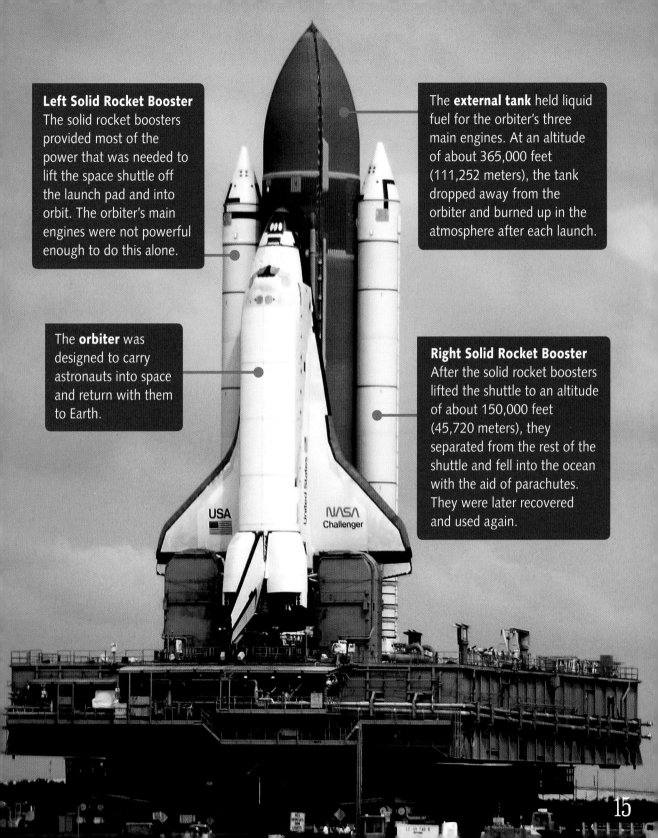

Left Solid Rocket Booster
The solid rocket boosters provided most of the power that was needed to lift the space shuttle off the launch pad and into orbit. The orbiter's main engines were not powerful enough to do this alone.

The **external tank** held liquid fuel for the orbiter's three main engines. At an altitude of about 365,000 feet (111,252 meters), the tank dropped away from the orbiter and burned up in the atmosphere after each launch.

The **orbiter** was designed to carry astronauts into space and return with them to Earth.

Right Solid Rocket Booster
After the solid rocket boosters lifted the shuttle to an altitude of about 150,000 feet (45,720 meters), they separated from the rest of the shuttle and fell into the ocean with the aid of parachutes. They were later recovered and used again.

USA

United States

NASA
Challenger

More Problems

Other factors contributed to the explosion. At 37 seconds into the flight, the shuttle experienced the first of several severe wind gusts. The wind created a stream of flames, causing increasing damage to the right-hand SRB. Just before the minute mark, videotapes of the flight showed smoke and flames on the right-side booster. Internal pressure in that booster dropped. The hole in the failed joint grew rapidly. Seconds later the flames caused the external fuel tank to collapse.

At 66 seconds videos showed bright spots on the side of the rocket facing the belly of the orbiter. At the time Mission Control and the *Challenger* crew did not realize anything was wrong.

At 72 seconds the joint linking the SRB and external tank broke. Massive amounts of liquid **hydrogen** and liquid oxygen escaped from the external tank. At almost the same time, several fireballs combined. An explosion rocked the area where the SRBs attached. Flames spread to the crew compartment where the astronauts sat.

hydrogen—a colorless gas that is lighter than air and burns easily

This ball of gas was created when the liquid hydrogen and oxygen inside the external tank ignited. The SRBs can be seen crossing paths.

Grounding the Shuttle

At 73 seconds the shuttle was traveling just under twice the speed of sound. It had reached a height of 46,000 feet (14,000 meters). The orbiter section broke into pieces and fell back to Earth. All seven astronauts on board died. Some may have died instantly. Others probably survived until the crew compartment crashed into the ocean almost three minutes later.

The crew compartment is visible in this image taken 78 seconds after liftoff. When it hit the Atlantic Ocean, the compartment was traveling more than 200 miles (321 kilometers) per hour.

People all over the world reacted in shock. The fact that a civilian had died made the tragedy seem even worse. The *Challenger* disaster had far-reaching effects. NASA grounded the shuttle program for two and a half years. Engineers worked to correct the O-ring design flaw that had allowed the fuel leakage. Meanwhile, NASA put new safety regulations in place. They hoped to prevent similar tragedies in the future.

Parts of the *Challenger* space shuttle were recovered in the Atlantic Ocean.

The Rogers Commission's final report announced two major problems in the *Challenger* tragedy. The first was the failure of the O-rings. The seals failed to prevent hot gases from leaking through the joint as the rocket propellant burned. The commission determined that the O-ring failure was caused by "a faulty design."

The solution was to produce a safer O-ring. After the accident NASA and MTI redesigned the entire SRB. The new design included three O-rings instead of two. An onboard heater was built into the joints to keep the O-rings from getting too cold. Engineers also used a stronger material and added a heating strip to the new O-rings.

The report also said poor communication among team members was a big problem. Disagreements between engineers and supervisors were not communicated to NASA officials. The report found the final decision to launch questionable. "If the decision-makers had known all of the facts," said the report, "it is highly unlikely that they would have decided to launch."

MTI ASSESSMENT OF TEMPERATURE CONCERN ON SRM-25 (51L) LAUNCH

O CALCULATIONS SHOW THAT SRM-25 O-RINGS WILL BE 20° COLDER THAN SRM-15 O-RINGS

O TEMPERATURE DATA NOT CONCLUSIVE ON PREDICTING PRIMARY O-RING BLOW-BY

O ENGINEERING ASSESSMENT IS THAT:

    O COLDER O-RINGS WILL HAVE INCREASED EFFECTIVE DUROMETER ("HARDER")

    O "HARDER" O-RINGS WILL TAKE LONGER TO "SEAT"

        O MORE GAS MAY PASS PRIMARY O-RING BEFORE THE PRIMARY SEAL SEATS (RELATIVE TO SRM-15)

           O DEMONSTRATED SEALING THRESHOLD IS 3 TIMES GREATER THAN 0.038" EROSION EXPERIENCED ON SRM-15

    O IF THE PRIMARY SEAL DOES NOT SEAT, THE SECONDARY SEAL WILL SEAT

        O PRESSURE WILL GET TO SECONDARY SEAL BEFORE THE METAL PARTS ROTATE

           O O-RING PRESSURE LEAK CHECK PLACES SECONDARY SEAL IN OUTBOARD POSITION WHICH MINIMIZES SEALING TIME

O MTI RECOMMENDS STS-51L LAUNCH PROCEED ON 28 JANUARY 1986

    O SRM-25 WILL NOT BE SIGNIFICANTLY DIFFERENT FROM SRM-15

JOE C. KILMINSTER, VICE PRESIDENT
SPACE BOOSTER PROGRAMS

MORTON THIOKOL, INC.
Wasatch Division

This document outlines MTI's reasons for going ahead with the *Challenger* launch on January 28, 1986, despite the forecast. It mentions the negative effect of cold temperatures on the primary O-rings. It also states that the secondary O-rings would not be negatively affected and would seal correctly, making the launch safe.

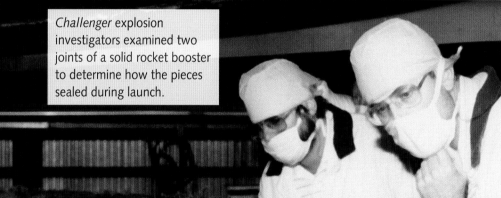

Challenger explosion investigators examined two joints of a solid rocket booster to determine how the pieces sealed during launch.

Pressure suits contain oxygen tanks and a supply of water.

Safety First

The commission suggested communication between engineers and NASA officials needed improvement. NASA worked to lessen the pressures that could lead to "go fever." They wanted to make safety more important than schedules. Officials approved the *Challenger* launch because there was no firm evidence that it would be dangerous. NASA wanted to flip that thinking. Future decisions should be made based on firm evidence that a launch would be safe.

Everyone vowed to make future flights as safe as possible. In addition to redesigning the SRBs, NASA put in place other safety measures suggested by the commission. For instance, future astronauts would wear pressure suits with survival backpacks for launch and landing. Engineers also worked to design a crew escape system for orbiters. That way, astronauts would have a chance to get out in case of an emergency.

Finally, NASA felt ready to continue missions. They believed the shuttle had been made as safe as possible. On September 29, 1988, the space shuttle *Discovery* roared into space. Its mission was declared the "Return to Flight."

The *Discovery* space shuttle completed nearly 40 missions.

Space travel is no easy mission. Making repairs inside the craft is difficult. Making outside repairs in zero gravity is even harder. Rescue from crews on Earth is nearly impossible.

With those dangers in mind, engineers and scientists design and build spacecraft to be as safe as possible. Astronauts train for up to two years. Despite these precautions, accidents still occur. The *Challenger* crew members weren't the first or last astronauts to lose their lives.

Apollo 1

On January 27, 1967, the interior of the *Apollo 1* space capsule caught fire while it was on the ground during training. Three astronauts, Virgil I. Grissom, Edward H. White, and Roger B. Chaffee, died in this tragic accident. A final report after this disaster led the way to major design changes in NASA's testing methods and safety requirements.

Grissom, White, and Chaffee (left to right) sit inside a practice capsule. The accident that killed them took place the day after this photo was taken.

Among the many problems with the *Apollo 1* space capsule was an escape hatch that was difficult to use, making it hard for the astronauts to exit quickly. Another problem was the poorly installed electrical wiring. This created a spark that immediately ignited the pure oxygen inside the capsule.

Soyuz 11

In 1971 three cosmonauts aboard *Soyuz 11* died from lack of oxygen when a breathing **ventilation** valve ruptured in space. The spacecraft returned safely to Earth. It was only when the recovery crew opened the capsule that they discovered the cosmonauts had died. These cosmonauts were the only people who have truly died in outer space.

The *Challenger* crew members were the first astronauts to die during an actual mission. They had not yet left Earth's atmosphere, so they didn't really die in outer space.

ventilation—a system that allows the flow of fresh air

Georgi Dobrovolski, Vladislav Volkov, and Viktor Patsayev (left to right) would have survived the lack of oxygen and sudden decrease of pressure inside *Soyuz 11* if they had been wearing space suits.

HONORING THE CHALLENGER CREW

In March 1986 seven asteroids were named after each member of the *Challenger* crew. In 2004 the *Opportunity* rover's landing spot on Mars was named "The *Challenger* Memorial Station" in honor of the seven astronauts.

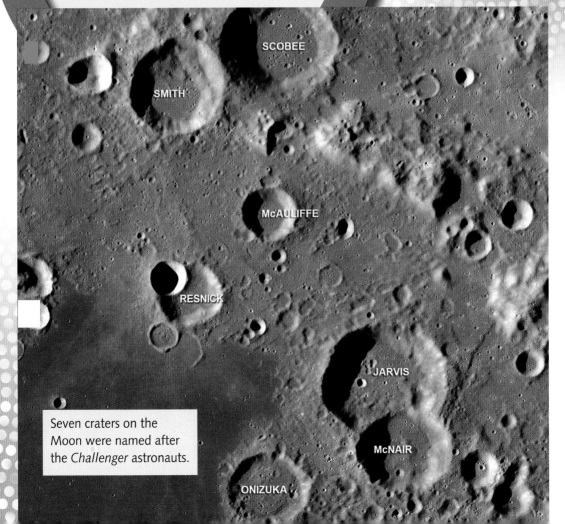

SCOBEE

SMITH

McAULIFFE

RESNICK

JARVIS

McNAIR

ONIZUKA

Seven craters on the Moon were named after the *Challenger* astronauts.

Tragedy Strikes Again

After *Challenger* the U.S. space program went for more than 10 years without another fatality. Then on February 1, 2003, another tragedy occurred. The orbiter *Columbia* broke apart as it returned to Earth after a successful mission in space. Just after takeoff a piece of foam broke off from the external fuel tank. It struck the orbiter's left wing and caused a small opening. The opening allowed gases to bleed into the orbiter as it made its re-entry into Earth's atmosphere two weeks later. The orbiter broke apart over Louisiana and Texas. All seven crew members died. They were the last astronauts to die as part of the shuttle program.

Despite safety suits, astronauts on *Columbia* were killed upon re-entry.

Lasting Effects

Christa McAuliffe

The space shuttle program ended in 2011. Two of NASA's orbiters were destroyed in accidents. The others were growing old and were expensive to operate.

Despite advances in safety, space travel remains dangerous. Since space travel began, just over 500 people have gone into space. Of those, 30 astronauts and cosmonauts have died either during spaceflight or training. The high rate of injury and death makes being an astronaut the world's most dangerous job. Despite the risks, the rewards of a successful mission are far greater.

"I touch the future. I teach," said Teacher in Space Christa McAuliffe before the *Challenger* flight. Decades later the bravery of the *Challenger* crew continues to touch and inspire people throughout the world.

DID YOU KNOW...?

In 2007 teacher-astronaut Barbara R. Morgan completed an 11-day mission on *Endeavor*. Morgan originally served as McAuliffe's backup in 1986.

commission (kuh-MI-shun)—a group of people gathered to complete an official task

compartment (kuhm-PART-muhnt)—a section or part of something

compress (kuhm-PRES)—to squeeze together into less space

cosmonaut (KAHZ-moh-nawt)—a Russian astronaut

debris (duh-BREE)—the pieces of something that has been broken

engineer (en-juh-NEER)—a person who uses science and math to plan, design, or build

erosion (i-ROH-zhuhn)—gradually worn away

hydrogen (HYE-druh-juhn)—a colorless gas that is lighter than air and burns easily

malfunction (mal-FUHNGK-shun)—a failure to work correctly

NASA—the government agency that runs the U.S. space program; stands for National Aeronautics and Space Administration

orbiter (OR-bit-ur)—the main part of a space shuttle; the orbiter is the part of the shuttle that goes into space and returns to Earth

propellant (pruh-PEL-uhnt)—fuel used in rocket motors

ventilation (ven-tuh-LAY-shuhn)—a system that allows the flow of fresh air

Internet Sites

FactHound offers a safe, fun way to find Internet sites related to this book. All of the sites on FactHound have been researched by our staff.

Here's all you do:

Visit *www.facthound.com*

Type in this code: 9781491420461

Super-cool stuff! Check out projects, games and lots more at **www.capstonekids.com**

1. Look at the timeline on pages 10–11. How long was the space shuttle *Challenger*'s launch time delayed? What does this suggest about the weather conditions that day? (Craft and Structure)

2. Describe the O-ring malfunction that occurred during liftoff and how it contributed to the *Challenger* disaster. (Key Idea and Details)

3. What effects did the *Challenger* disaster have on future shuttle missions? Support your answer with facts from the text as well as from research from print and online sources. (Integration of Knowledge and Ideas)

Read More

Baxter, Roberta. *The Challenger Explosion.* History's Greatest Disasters. Minneapolis: ABDO, 2013.

Holden, Henry. *Space Shuttle Disaster: The Tragic Mission of the Challenger.* Berkeley Heights, N.J.: Enslow, 2013.

Radomski, Kassandra. *The Apollo 13 Mission: Core Events of a Crisis in Space.* What Went Wrong? North Mankato: Capstone, 2014.

Index